650 | Back to High School

Edited by Edward McCann

650 | WHERE WRITERS READ

Founder / Editor • Edward McCann
Executive Producer • Richard Kollath
Literary Ombudsman • Steven Lewis
Chief of Operations • Jane Kaupp
Technical Advisor • Conrad Trautmann
Technical Advisor • Stephen Kaupp
Director of Communications • Gretchen Reed
Director of Photography • Kevin O'Connor
Videography/Photography • Sara Caldwell
Chief Audio Engineer • Jesse Chason
Copy Editor • Shelley Sadler Kenney
Graphic Designer • Diane Fokas
Production Director Emeritus • Gregory Bray

Production Assistants

Christopher Dennison, Diane Fokas, Mackenzie Meeks,
Jackie Mercurio, and Brian Reagher

Editorial Committee

Rachel Aydt, Laura Shaine Cunningham, Angela Davis-Gardner,
Joseph Goodrich, Steven Lewis, David Masello, and Honor Molloy

For all of our teachers, past and present.

ABOUT 650

Jocks. Nerds. Stoners. Does the mere thought of High School—and your former classmates—fill you with fond nostalgia, or a kind of creeping dread? Steven King wrote, "At the time we're stuck in it, like hostages locked in a Turkish bath, high school seems like the most serious business in the world. It's not until the second or third class reunion that we start realizing how absurd the whole thing was."

High School is a cocoon of sorts, a place where larval adolescents transition into young adults. It's a confusing metamorphosis that can be energizing or exhausting, humiliating or thrilling. This volume contains a sampling of those experiences from a select group of talented writers featured at a live reading at the New Rochelle Library in New York's Westchester County.

650 is a celebration of writing and the spoken word—a literary forum featuring two-page, 650-word personal stories that can be performed in five minutes. Our events at theaters, colleges, and libraries around the country are organized around single, broad topics that invite a range of expression, and recorded performances are added to a digital archive of writers reading their work aloud. The writers and their work receive additional exposure through podcasts, broadcasts, our YouTube channel, and in these printed volumes.

650 features graduate students and grandparents, first-timers and bestsellers. It's all about the writing, with an emphasis on craft. It's about the choice of one word over another, about the shape of sentences and paragraphs, the arc of a narrative, the poetry of a unique literary voice. If you love language and enjoy a good story, you've come to the right place. To submit your work or attend our shows, visit our website or Facebook page, and join our mailing list. Please tell your friends about us, and **spread the word about the spoken word.**

Ed McCann

Edward McCann, Founder / Editor

READ650.COM
FACEBOOK.COM/READ650

CONTENTS

650 | Back to High School

Edited by Edward McCann

JULIE TRELSTAD

Julie Trelstad is the Director of Julie Ink Creative Author Consulting, an agency specializing in helping authors grow their online presence. An expert in book publishing, Julie has spent two decades on the frontlines of the digital publishing frontier. For most of her career, Julie was an acquisitions editor for homebuilding, architecture, and construction books working at various publishers including Reader's Digest, The Taunton Press, and John Wiley & Sons. She's best known for acquiring the book, *The Not So Big House* by Sarah Susanka. Julie founded the Plain White Press, a non-fiction publishing company based in White Plains, NY, which she sold to Fox Chapel Publishing. Before founding Julie Ink, Julie spent several years at Writers House, a literary agency where she managed the agency's digital publishing program. When she's not dancing or helping authors, Julie is currently finishing her first novel.

MY FIRST FROG

Julie Trelstad

Pretty wasn't my thing. I was a smart girl, and my limited experience with boys had led me to believe that Kansas guys weren't interested in smart. At sixteen, I'd determined that I'd never have a boyfriend, even though I wanted one.

I hoped things might turn around at summer debate camp, where a quick mind would surely win over a curvy body. But hopes were dashed when every guy slobbered over my gorgeous red-headed roommate, Wendy. Every guy except John Lawson, the small-town boy randomly assigned to be my partner.

John was the top debater from Satanta, Kansas, population twelve hundred. I'd never heard of it. He described it as an oil town south and west of Dodge City—an area of the state so desolate you wouldn't go out driving without a spare container of gas in the trunk.

John stood six feet tall and had pimply skin, wavy blond hair, and wire-frame glasses a decade out of style. His wide mouth reminded me of a frog.

I liked frogs. I'd been acquiring toy frogs and figurines since elementary school. I carried a desiccated frog left over from AP Bio in my debate briefcase for good luck. The school newspaper even ran a

1

feature on me and my frog collection, which may have been another reason I had yet to go on a date.

I told John he looked like my good luck frog. I hadn't exactly meant it as a compliment, but he answered by telling me he thought I was cute.

Then he asked me to his prom. In Satanta. Three hundred and thirty miles from Topeka.

Using his keen debate skills, John argued that I needed to join him because there were not enough girls for all the guys in Satanta. We didn't have to go steady.

He didn't need to argue. I was thunderstruck. I liked John okay, but I really liked him liking me. I would get to go to the Junior Prom! And I would fly in two planes (Topeka to Wichita, Wichita to Dodge City) to get there. If I screwed up my first attempt at romance, none of my Topeka friends, who were already pairing off, would be the wiser.

My mom took me to Kansas City to buy a dress. I chose a one-of-a-kind white column of satin with pink, peach, and turquoise organza ruffles at the shoulder that made me feel sexy.

When I arrived in Satanta, John's mother helped me apply half a can of Aquanet to my permed and electric-rollered hair. She warned me that my cultivated curls would whip around my face in the fierce prairie wind if I didn't use it. I closed my eyes and let her spray. By the time she was finished, my hair bounced stiffly like wheat ready for harvest. With some sparkly aqua-blue eyeshadow and peach lip gloss, I felt transformed—like Sandy in Grease.

John and I emerged from the gym sweaty and high from dancing into inky darkness. A strong wind pushed the clouds away but didn't ruffle my hair. Tiny stars—more than I'd ever seen with my bare eyes—sparkled in the vast sky. I wished I wanted to be there with John, but I needed to escape his incessant talk about cars, sports, and comic books.

He smelled like Clearasil when I finally let him kiss me with his dry lips. I didn't feel fireworks. John bored me. He wasn't the prince I had hoped for.

Disappointed I didn't want to make out, he helped me arrange my frothy dress in the front seat of his red convertible, so it wouldn't get stuck in the door. We drove to Main Street to cruise between the town's two stoplights honking, waving, and squealing to the other prom-goers. John smiled his wide frog smile as he showed me off, his smart, pretty date from the big city.

BRUCE SHENITZ

Bruce Shenitz is a writer, editor, librarian, content strategist, and taxonomist—usually not all at the same time. His reporting and essays have appeared in *Out*, the *New York Times*, the *Los Angeles Times Magazine*, *Newsweek*, and several anthologies. He is the editor of the essay anthology, *The Man I Might Become: Gay Men Write About Their Fathers*, which won a Lambda Literary Award.

OUTSIDERS

Bruce Shenitz

Jennie and I had just come from a Jimi Hendrix concert at Madison Square Garden. "Don't come any closer to my building," Jennie said, as we embraced on the dark city street. "My grandmother would kill me if she knew I'd been out with a boy—especially a white boy."

Jennie lived with her grandparents in public housing just four blocks but a world away from my middle-class apartment building in Peter Cooper Village. She was Chinese-American, I was moderately observant Jewish, and her immigrant grandparents were very old-country.

We were a sort of updated West Side Story. Except we lived on the east side. And, more importantly, although Jennie might have been my high school girlfriend in a parallel universe, it wasn't going to happen in this one. I already suspected I might be gay, so the complicated logistics of our night with Jimi Hendrix were just another way that our relationship was unconventional.

We had met at Junior High School 104 and were an unlikely pair: she was poor, worked after school and on weekends as a supermarket cashier, and was a de facto orphan because of a complicated family situation. I lived with two parents in economic security at a time when being a middle-class Manhattanite was not an oxymoron. My social calendar was filled with piano lessons, Hebrew school, playground punch ball games, and bar mitzvah receptions. Jennie believed that some of the Stuyvesant Town and Peter Cooper Village girls looked down on her for not having the "right clothes," and though she gave me credit for not being a snob, she did chide me for being a bit spoiled. And while school was relatively easy for me, she did well by force of will and hard work.

I'm still not quite sure why we became friends at first—we both may have guessed that the other was a bit of an outsider— or how we stayed fast friends at Stuyvesant High School. But we were fascinated by our different backgrounds, teaching one another words in Cantonese, Hebrew, and Yiddish. I do know that we talked on the phone for hours at a time. I also remember that my parents seemed alternately puzzled and mildly disturbed by our friendship. Maybe they suspected that my friend-who-is-a-girl-but-not-my-girlfriend foreshadowed a gay future. They'd met Jennie a couple of times when she came over to the apartment, and while they were always polite, they didn't seem to quite welcome her.

At the time I didn't understand their coolness toward Jennie. Then my grandmother sat me down and explained the dueling facts of life: on the one hand, people liked to stay with their own kind; on the other, "Those shiksas are trained to go after Jewish men because they make the best husbands." I often repeated that line to my lapsed-Catholic husband, and it never failed to provoke an eye-roll, as if to say, "Whatever grandma may have told you, you're not all that.

I might have figured out the score earlier, but even in post-Stonewall New York, no one talked much about gay people. Self-knowledge came slowly, often only when looking back. I didn't understand until years later why I remembered a certain water balloon fight so vividly. A group of us were gleefully attacking each other with the loaded balloons one day after school was over. Our wet shirts and pants enticingly revealed the bodies that lay beneath.

Later, during one of our marathon Friday night phone calls, I got Jennie to keep repeating that "all the girls thought that Jimmy looked so cute now that he'd switched to contact lenses and cut his Beatles-length hair."

Even though she was one of my closest friends, I couldn't yet articulate to myself that I felt the same way, much less say the words out loud. So, I let her speak them for me.

IRENE O'GARDEN

Irene O'Garden has won or been nominated for prizes in nearly every writing category from stage to e-screen, hardcovers, as well as literary magazines and anthologies. She's the winner of a Pushcart Prize, and her critically-acclaimed play *Women On Fire*, played sold-out houses at Off-Broadway's Cherry Lane Theatre and was nominated for a Lucille Lortel Award. Her essays have been featured in dozens of literary journals and award-winning anthologies, and her first poetry collection, *Fulcrum*, was published in 2017 by Nirala. Harper published her first memoir *Fat Girl*; her second, *Risking the Rapids: How My Wilderness Journey Healed my Childhood* is forthcoming from Mango in 2019. She is joyfully married to writer John Pielmeier.

BFF

Irene O'Garden

I spent my grade school years without friends. As a fat teacher's pet in a wrinkled ink-stained blouse, I had too many strikes against me. Shy around classmates, I sunk into books, wondering where was the Piglet to my Pooh, the Charlotte to my Wilbur?

But hormones must have psychological equivalents. Entering high school, my gland of intuition secreted a radical decision: "Even though I'm fat, I won't be shy anymore."

The hallway is the Times Square of high school, and passing through it, I greet everyone, even those from grade school. Coining nicknames, magnanimous, driving my personality through the halls like a brand new '66 Pontiac.

I Get Involved. Clean-up? I'm there. Chorus? I'm in. Plan the St. Patrick's Assembly? You betcha.

In 1966, Batman is all over the airwaves. Tossing around skit ideas for the Assembly, I say, "What about 'Patman' and Robin?" The Committee laughs. Acceptance!

"He could fight 'Big Orange,'" ventures Erin, another freshman. (Orange is anathema on St Paddy's Day.) Who is that? She gets my humor.

Another idea. "What if..." Then she says, "And we could..."

"...then Patman says..." Two musicians jamming for the first time.

We can't scribble the script fast enough.

At the Assembly, a gymnasium of whooping laughter greets our closing line. We're a hit!

I'm especially glad to greet Erin in the halls. She loves words, she's funny. She doesn't seem to mind that I'm fat or that my hair's not as pretty as hers.

As the year unfolds, we exchange vacation postcards and summer phone calls. We seek each other out the first day of school and before long, we create a weekly comic broadcast over the school's PA system. Hidden behind a microphone, I unleash my performing self, too.

And Erin has a car.

Oh, the blessed independence of that old blue Dodge! A place to talk, a place to take us places, I to her house, she to mine. Out, out, away, away from our mothers, our teachers, our spiteful acquaintances. Off to rehearsal, to art fairs, to Sears, or to silence. Junk-food wrappers flapping on the floor, bits of scripts, yearbook layouts, calculator paper we unroll and fly like kites.

We become the best of friends. Teach each other how to listen, how to give a good gift, how to develop insight. How to love another person.

Years later, I spot a doppelgänger of her old blue Dodge in a shopping center parking lot. Same rust eating at the bent-up fenders. Same blue upholstery with the fraying edge. Same blue metal steering wheel and metal knobs and rods. Same circular speedometer that racked up all our miles.

I stand there and see us in our winter coats, our summer shorts, our party clothes. I see us doubled and quadrupled up in laughter, foreheads bumping on the metal dash. I see the wads of tear-sopped Kleenex in the ashtray. Malts spilling in the heater as our hearts spilled out.

I think of all the nights and lakes and early mornings and waterfalls that windshield held. Of the futures we drew beneath that map-light. The questions, the answers, the songs.

This car isn't Erin's. Hers burned up in college, thanks to me. On our way to visit a hospitalized friend, I flicked my cigarette out the front window. Returning to the blackened hull, we realized that my discarded cigarette had flown into the open back window, incinerating the car while we visited our friend. A Viking funeral.

This Dodge was but a metal ghost. Still, I almost felt a perfect right to jump into my old accustomed place, in that compartment of harmony, watching her driving profile transporting us our separate ways into adulthood.

Best friends forever? Nothing about high school is forever.

SHARON FORMAN

Raised in Norfolk, Virginia, **Sharon Forman** is a reform rabbi who has worked for twenty-four years in the field of Jewish education. She is the author of *Honest Answers to your Child's Jewish Questions*, a chapter in Lisa Grushcow's *The Sacred Encounter: Jewish Perspectives on Sexuality*, and most recently, *The Baseball Haggadah: A Festival of Freedom and Springtime in 15 Innings*. Forman has also written for *Mothers Always Write, Kveller, Mamalode, Literary Mama*, and the *Union for Reform Judaism website, The Bitter Southerner, Lilith.org*, and *Parent. co*. She lives with her husband and three children in Westchester County, New York where she teaches Bar and Bat Mitzvah students.

WAY BACK

Sharon Forman

By the time I reached eleventh grade, my older brother had taken control of our family's battered Buick station wagon and drove us to school each day in enforced silence. He agreed to take my friend, Lisa, with the blonde layered bangs, but ultimately banished another classmate from the backseat who committed the offense of chatting in the soft hours just after 7a.m. During my senior year after my brother had graduated, I avoided the morning school bus when my best friend bought a green Dodge Dart and bartered rides for token contributions of gas money.

Ninth and tenth grade, however, involved daily trips on Miss Hattie's school bus, with its identification badge proudly displayed in her windshield like the number of a church hymn. She transported us to the building noted for its porthole-sized windows and its eerie similarity to the Norfolk, Virginia city jail, with which it shared an architect and similar measures of charm.

During those two years, Miss Hattie was often the first adult who greeted me each school day. Decked out in crocheted flat hats in pastel colors, Miss Hattie opened the bus doors brimming with energy and purpose. With her giant, plastic eyeglass frames, Miss Hattie resembled an owl with a deep mocha complexion. At the tender age of fifteen, I appreciated Miss Hattie's predictability and reassuring daily appearance. My father frequently left early for breakfast meetings, and my mother was not a creature of the morning. Still tireless at midnight—writing letters, separating loads of laundry, balancing the checkbook, or packing up goody bags to deliver to family and friends for any of a number of Jewish holidays, my mom avoided dawn like the Transylvanian vampires rumored to fly around my family tree. I avoided waking up my mom unless I was scheduled to take an important test, in which case she insisted on dragging herself downstairs wrapped in a petal pink bathrobe, defying her circadian rhythms to prepare a breakfast of scrambled eggs for me—which would guarantee maximum brain function due to "the protein." Maintaining adequate levels of protein was an underutilized and secret tool in achieving academic success, according to my mother.

Fortified by a bowl of Wheat Chex and Jane Pauley's rendition of the morning headlines, my brother and I headed out to the bus stop, waiting for Miss Hattie's golden chariot. The creaky doors opened, and Miss Hattie would clap her hands and belt out verses to gospel music, as she greeted us and the other sour-faced members of her captive congregation. "Blessed Day to you!" she would intone like a benediction. Being Jewish, I had never experienced this particular type of praying. The Catholic kids on the bus looked somewhat perplexed, as well. "Way back," she serenaded us. I understood that we needed to find seats in the rear, where you could feel the whirring electrical system of the vehicle. My big brother thought she was suggesting that we travel to God or even Jesus, but neither of us ever once told our mother about Miss Hattie's church singing, as we didn't want to get her in trouble. Way back in the

1970's, my mom had calmly confronted the pious principal of our public elementary school with something called the Establishment Clause and single-handedly ended daily forced recitations of "The Lord's Prayer." We weren't risking Miss Hattie's blurring the lines between church and school bus.

On Miss Hattie's chariot we rolled through neighborhood streets named for fragrant trees and bushes: Magnolia, Mimosa, and Camellia. If not to Canaan, Miss Hattie sang us all the way to high school. The Hebrew Blessings for the Dawn may be etched way back into the mitochondria of my cells, but since high school, they have been joined by the beating of Miss Hattie's wide-open hands clapping her joyous morning song.

JOHN MITCHELL MORRIS

John Mitchell Morris earned his MFA in Creative Writing at Sarah Lawrence College, his JD from Villanova University School of Law, and his BA from California State University, Northridge. His novel-in-progress, *In the Trembling Heart*, is a love story set in the early twenty-first century and explores the intersections of tragedy, art, and redemption. A former actor, Morris appeared in *Showtime's Queer as Folk*, *NBC's E-Ring*, and *Todd Stephen's Another Gay Movie*. He is a member of the State Bar of California and practiced law in Los Angeles. Morris is presently a lecturer in writing at Purchase College, State University of New York. He lives in New York City.

THE MINORS

John Mitchell Morris

The Shoretown, Texas curfew for minors began Fridays at midnight. But at 1:00 a.m., our arms cradled toilet paper and nine dozen eggs as we leapt from Nolan's fence and darted across the wheat field toward East Dune Elementary. Only Nolan had attended East Dune, but that was years ago. He, Howdy, and I were freshman now, and after our first hometown football game, we'd stashed our band uniforms in Nolan's room and plotted our break to April Ashleigh's house. As a junior, cheerleader, and drum major, April Ashleigh had little use for our names. "Hi Boys," were the scraps on which we lived. But egging her car and streaming miles of toilet tissue across her father's crape myrtles felt vital to our hopeless adoration.

"Slow down!" Howdy whisper-shouted. At fourteen years old, he had yet to reach five feet tall.

"Hurry up!" Nolan said.

Stealthily, I passed them, quiet and quick on my feet.

We reached East Dune and tiptoed down the tin-roofed corridors. I had never left my bedroom after curfew, much less

17

trespassed on government property. I felt grown now. Free. But when we turned the C-wing corner, the scene across the courtyard broke our stride. In a faint pool of moonlight, April Ashleigh crouched against a metal beam. Her sobs echoed off the concrete, and her t-shirt hung loose—maybe torn?—off her shoulder. A muscular figure towered above her. We recognized him even without his last name spelled across his back: Chavez. Hours earlier, he'd strutted across the end zone; now he stood still and ominous. He mumbled something and reached for her. April shook her head and said, "No."

We did not move. Then Nolan, with a courage I envied and cursed, yelled, "Leave her alone!"

They turned to us. But before either responded, a bright light flashed on our backs and voices called from the distance: "Police! Freeze!" In the glare, I saw only pistols.

As instructed, we surrendered our tissue and eggs and raised high our hands. We pointed and pleaded, insisting our friend was in trouble. A flashlight scanned the corridor, but the emptiness fashioned us liars.

Handcuffed, we slid into the patrol car, begging, to no avail, that the officers find April and Chavez. Nolan fumed. Howdy sobbed. Doom swelled in my gut.

"What if he hit her?" I whispered.

"Or worse," Nolan replied.

"What if he's killing her right now?" Howdy cried.

The officers hushed us, and we reached the station—and our cell—in silence.

On Monday morning, we met in the band hall. As witnesses to a crime, we agreed to accompany each other everywhere. But in the foyer before the first bell, we came to face-to-face with April Ashleigh. She stopped and looked at us, but offered no "Hi, Boys." Then she shouldered her way to the stairwell, glancing back to find us watching.

Fifteen years later, while posting pictures on Facebook, I received a message from Chavez.

"You probably don't remember me," he writes, followed by something about Shoretown High.

"I remember you," I reply.

Then after a moment he types, "It wasn't what you think."

I am stunned. I respond: "That night has so tortured my imagination, whatever actually happened would probably disappoint me."

"It won't," he assures. "I wanted to tell you then but couldn't. Do you want to know?"

I hesitate before typing YED. In my anticipation, I have forgotten how to spell.

There is a pause, followed by the flicker of gray ellipses that indicate he is writing. Two minutes. Five. Ten. They vanish, and an endless blue box appears. I absorb it as if all at once. The words seem gigantic in their shaming of my wildest fantasies, revealing how far from adulthood Nolan, Howdy, and I had stood that night, with nothing but a prank on our minds, when in front of us worlds were crumbling.

AMANDA CARGILL

Amanda Cargill is a Brooklyn-based writer specializing in short fiction and memoir. Her food, travel, culture and lifestyle features have appeared in domestic, multicultural and international publications.

BRIGHT WHITE COOL

Amanda Cargill

Her name was Rindi. Like Cindy—the name I insisted my schoolmates call me when we played "House" as girls—but different, better. Rindi was a high school senior when I was a freshman. She had thick, blond hair to her waist and boobs bigger than any I'd ever seen. I could hardly believe we were close enough in age to attend the same school; Rindi, with her seventeen-year-old curves, and me, a fourteen-year-old lollipop. She was Homecoming queen, and head cheerleader, and the most popular girl in school. I dreamed of one day being just like her.

I'd always had these sorts of fantasies—still do—of basking in the bright white spotlight of cool. When I was in the first grade, I idolized my sixteen-year-old neighbor, another cheerleader and the daughter of the winningest high school football coach in the history of our one-horse town. Every Saturday, I dragged my coloring books and crayons to our home's enormous front lawn and while pretending to draw, snuck furtive glances at Michelle and her cheerleader friends practicing their routines. I memorized every move, every shout, every clap, and after Michelle's friends left, made my four-year-old brother practice these moves and shouts and claps with me. Recognizing a talent, or more likely, an obsession, my mom enrolled me in a local cheerleader clinic. I was pretty good, but it didn't change the fact of my bowl haircut and gift for math, neither of which did my cool quotient any favors.

By my own senior year of high school, I'd made "girl next door" my trademark. I was cute in a Sally *Field Flying Nun* sort of way and had realized my dream of becoming a cheerleader, albeit the geeky one. Cool continued to elude me, which is why it was so baffling when Mike Wright, the coolest, cutest and meanest student at Stillwell High, nominated me for Homecoming queen.

It happened at the exceptionally well-attended senior class meeting that was held two weeks before the Homecoming football game. Every girl harboring her own Rindi dream was there. Mike raised his hand and when Mr. Forrester, the biology teacher famed for his monotone and complete and utter loathing of his job, called on him, he said "Amanda. I nominate Amanda."

I gasped, shocked both by the nomination and the sound of my name skittering for the first time across Mike's perfect lips.

Mr. Forrester wrote my name on the chalkboard alongside a handful of others. Votes were cast anonymously by a show of hands; students closed their eyes and pressed their foreheads into the pillow-shaped cushion that resulted from resting a single, rounded forearm on their desks. When the voting was done, I raised my head and saw my name, the only name, on the chalkboard.

Me? I was the official senior class nominee for Homecoming queen? Me?... Me... Me!!! Unable to help myself, I smiled a too big smile. *How could it be?* Inside of three minutes, I'd become cool, basking, at last, in the glow of the bright, white spotlight I'd dreamt of my entire life.

I never asked Mike why he nominated me. At the time, as now, I was shocked that he knew I existed. But I remain forever grateful. Whatever the reason, he put me as close to cool as I've ever been, and kids, no matter what your parents tell you about it "not being important what other people think..." They're lying. The bright white light of cool shines on everyone at least once or twice. Maybe not in high school. Maybe not in college. In fact, you might have to wait until your wedding day or your book launch party or the night you roll into the class reunion with the hottest person in the room on your arm. But when you do, you'll know.

OLIVIA GRAYSON

Olivia Grayson creates prose and poetry that combine pop culture with autobiography. Her poetry has been published in journals such as *The Birds We Piled Loosely, BlazeVOX, Bombay Gin, Fourth & Sycamore, Requited Journal,* and others. She has also recorded and published her writing on Talking Book. Olivia teaches and writes in Brooklyn, New York.

AUTUMNAL MEMORY

Olivia Grayson

It was there, in damp suburbia, the early morning sun veiled by tricky clouds, that I plodded on, crushing the netted veins of saturated leaves that covered the sidewalks in golden-ruby layers.

I breathed in the smell of moist earth, tinged with last night's rows and rows of chimney smoke, clouds of tar oil and ash merged and suspended.

I breathed deeper; something piercing and rank: dog shit, and I was standing in it, incessant and dismal; I was standing in it, and the school bus pulled up.

I entered dumb, dumb as the as the door that flailed open and smacked shut behind me, when some pink-faced kid cried out: *Is that Grayson? Oh my God; it is! She stepped in shit!"*

"Go home, go home, go home…"

I thought the command was coming from inside my head, but it was Mark Laurenella the darling, the heartthrob, the button nosed and cupid's lips, and I had stepped in shit.

I stood motionless; punch-drunk. It was as if I had too many limbs and forgot which ones I was meant to use.

It was then the bus driver left his seat and physically ushered me out, back to the site of my betrayer, the golden-ruby, double-crossing pavement, every dog in the neighborhood my enemy now, as I frantically pushed down on the heels of my crap-laden All Stars, kicking like a deranged showgirl, until they flew off, one landing atop a Little Bluestem shrub, its reeds splitting open upon impact.

Freed of the vices that had gripped me, I raced home sweaty, angry, humiliated.

Once there, I dumped the entire contents of my backpack, grabbed the fattest textbook I had—the1,540-page *Introduction to Literature*—and slammed it with white-hot rage against the front door, hysterically reciting the broad themes embedded in my 15 year-old brain: Evil! Tyranny! God! Alienation! Uncertainty! Revenge! Power! Death! Mother!

Mother.

I charged inside and planted myself at her bedside where she was recuperating from the latest round of chemotherapy and radiation treatment poisoning her so she would be cured.

I longed for her to feel my outrage; to hold me; instead, she gazed blankly; her eyes held no expression.

Impetuosity, I flung myself upon her, and as I did, the bed dislodged from its frame and the leaden mattress drooped—half up, half down, a dire rectangle divided in two folds.

Mother flopped, in a crooked gray tangle, then she spoke,

"Go back to school, Debbie," and it had never been more essential to do what she told me, to give her that control.

I crawled off the wreck of bifurcated mattress and went to my room where I contemplated my feet—it might have been hours; it might have been seconds, then peeled off my shredded socks and put on fresh, soft white ones.

I told her goodbye.

School was unremarkable save for a few snickers and "P-U Debbies," which spiraled about me as I drifted shoeless through fifth and sixth period.

A previous version of "Autumnal Memories" has appeared in *The Grief Diaries*.

ANNABEL MONAGHAN

Annabel Monaghan is the author of two novels for young adults, *A Girl Named Digit* and *Double Digit*. She is also the author of *Does This Volvo Make My Butt Look Big?*, a collection of essays based on her column that appears on the *Huffington Post, The Week* and *The Rye Record*. She teaches novel writing at The Writing Institute at Sarah Lawrence College and lives in Rye, New York with her husband and three sons.

BACK TO SCHOOL NIGHT

Annabel Monaghan

The cool kids are hanging by the lockers, laughing and talking a little too loud. The nerds are in the classroom early, eager to shake hands with the teacher and nab the seats in the front row. The girls are put together in skinny jeans, heels, and blown-out hair. You know what I'm talking about, right? This is back-to-school night, and these are the parents of actual high schoolers.

Back-to-school night for high school is dramatically different than it is at elementary school. When you go to the little kids' school, you are acutely aware of your status as an adult. You sit in teeny tiny chairs and look through the "artwork" that your child has left for you. The teacher talks about how he's going to teach your kid to do stuff that you already know how to do. It's adorable how they're growing up, isn't it?

In contrast, back-to-school night at your kid's high school makes you feel like a kid. I wander from class to class with no clue as to where I'm going. The traffic in the halls is so socially overwhelming that I find myself saying hello to everyone like I'm running for student council president. Skinny Jeans walks by me

29

and flips her hair without saying hello. I wonder what that means. Did I say the wrong thing? Did I say the right thing but to the wrong person and it got back to her?

I am in a time warp and I've brought everyone with me. That guy who's texting in class—he was a note passer. That girl who's writing down every word the teacher says (even the jokes)—she's going to be valedictorian. The jock in the back row is stretching because he had a really hard practice today. And look, he's married to a cheerleader.

And just like in like high school, half the time I have no clue what the teachers are talking about. I walk into biology and the teacher has an assignment for us on the board. "Record your inferences about these photos." *Look, lady, I didn't come here to do homework.* You can't make me. One photo looks like a bunch of colors and the other looks like a feather. I write that down, grudgingly. She starts her presentation by telling us the answer. I wasn't even close. I swear, just like high school.

When it's time for break, I hit the cafeteria and am relieved to find my BFF. She seems relieved to find me too, and we move to a safe corner. It's loud and crowded and the popular girls are selling things behind a folding table, somehow already in a club. Skinny Jeans is there and looks sublimely happy. I have a feeling she feels like she's back in high school, too.

I am happy when the bell rings and I can go to English. This woman speaks my language. I telegraph to her from my seat in the very front of the class (I guess that settles it, I'm a nerd) how much I love her and every book she's teaching and how much I want to be her when I grow up. Even though she's 30. I leave without saying hello, however, because I don't trust myself to be cool about it.

I go to more classes, each eight minutes long. Calculus, as it turns out, has very few numbers and is too complicated for the teacher to explain to us. I'm a little grateful. The bell rings again and we check our schedules to figure out where our next class is. I have gym, so I instinctively run through my handy list of female problems that disarm male gym coaches. But then it hits me, I'm a grown up. I can just go home.

NETRA SREEPRAKASH

Netra Sreeprakash graduated from Vassar College, where she received the English Department Prize in Fiction, and Columbia Law School. She was born in Aurora and grew up in Littleton, Colorado and has been practicing law for over a decade.

BRIGHT, COLD

Netra Sreeprakash

I saw a headline in the computer room between classes, as I signed out of my e-mail (Hotmail). A shooting, a school in Colorado. This is embarrassing—I assumed it was in the inner-city. I had to get to class. I didn't even click on the link.

In class, someone asked me about it—I was the only Coloradoan in that school—and I had nothing to say, so at lunch, I swept past the canteen (a bold move) and sat down at a computer to catch up. I thought I might recognize the name of the school -- maybe one of those Denver schools named after old presidents: George Washington, Thomas Jefferson, Abraham Lincoln. I thought I'd see something about gangs.

Instead, I saw "Columbine." I started scanning for names I recognized, and too quickly, there was one. I devoured words. 25 suspected dead. Adolf Hitler's birthday. Nazis. Race. Aloud, I said, "Oh, D-, what did you do?"

I had been the only kid in that class in four years of elementary school who wasn't white (putting aside blonde K-, with her Cherokee grandmother). When we had to go around in fourth grade putting

33

every kid's name next to a descriptor listed on a sheet ("This person's initials spell a word," "This person has been in the hospital."), everyone assumed I was the one born in another country. J- was the foreign-born one, a Britisher. But she was brown-haired and played soccer. I, though born in Aurora, was far more foreign.

So maybe I was the only brown person he had really known. And I had not done enough to make us human. I remembered our independent study projects from third and fourth grade. He chose Lou Gehrig and then, when we did countries, Italy. He was in my presentation group, and we had sock puppets that dropped the names of our chosen countries into sentences. His puppet was an Italian chef, "Tally," and mine was a black-haired girl, "Dia." Ro (of Romania) and Dia said, "We want to eat, Tally." Eat-Tally, Italy. Tally invited us into his restaurant with a bow, "Come in, Dia." In-dia. We were not even embarrassed.

The sliding doors on the sides of the canteen were, as usual, all open to the humid air. In the kitchen, the stern Singaporean-Chinese cooks were plating and serving a Western dish, an Asian dish, a salad. My United World friends were gathered around circular tables on the near side. I stumbled to them. I opened my mouth, but as the words began to pour out, the sobs came. I fell to my knees on the brown tile floor. My friends, from Hong Kong, Italy, Japan, Norway, India, Holland, and Ethiopia, surrounded me as I wept.

Call home, someone suggested. My parents told me they had called friends, so many kids we knew. That boy had managed to walk home, called his mom and dad. That girl's family had recorded an outgoing message: she was safe and with her parents. How many calls were made, how many lines crossed?

In an island city-state, I disconnected the phone.

There were silhouettes on the walls of that high school. I remember, from district choir performances, from elementary school. Columbine Rebels. Not Confederate riffraff, but the Yankee founding fathers in tricorne hats, huddling, darting, battling Brits at every corridor. I recall dark blue outlines of muskets on whitewashed walls.

Maybe I imagined those.

But I had a real picture, in my collection from home. Our class in fifth grade, in some semblance of rows before a yellow JeffCo school bus. He, always one of the tallest kids in the class, was standing in the back, baseball cap on, head bowed—the only one not squinting toward the camera against the glare of the sun and the bright, cold snow.

ANN LEVIN

Ann Levin is a writer and editor. She worked for many years as a journalist at newspapers in Texas and California and at The Associated Press, for which she continues to write book reviews. In addition, she's contributed to articles to *AARP Bulletin* and other publications. She lives in New York City with her husband, Stan Honda, a photographer.

HELPLESSLY HOPING

Ann Levin

Their names were Monica, Margo, Nancy and Barbara, and they were the cool girls, the hip girls, the girls that all the boys loved in high school. And some of the teachers too. I hadn't thought about them for years until last summer, when I was reading a review of a new biography about the singer/songwriter Stephen Stills.

The writer was saying that no other musician's songs were woven as deeply into the hearts and minds and souls of the baby boomer generation as Stephen Stills'. And if you were to get a random assortment of us boomers together, we'd still be able to sing his biggest hits by heart. And not only that, but in harmony.

Really?, I thought. I hated Stephen Stills in high school, especially that infernal album simply titled Crosby, Stills and Nash, which Monica, Margo, Nancy and Barbara used to play all the time. The album where the three of them are sitting with their guitars on a broken-down couch outside a dilapidated house in their scuffed boots, faded jeans, and shaggy hair.

I wondered why this band had apparently transfixed my generation like no other, at least according to this writer. So I went online to listen to the songs she mentioned in the article, and the first one I clicked on was called "Helplessly Hoping." No sooner did I hear the first notes of Stephen Stills' acoustic guitar than I was transported back to the big, red brick girls' dormitory at the Quaker boarding school outside Philadelphia where I went to high school.

It was 1969 or '70, a sunny Saturday afternoon. "Helplessly Hoping" was blasting out of a dorm room, and Barbara was gliding down the hall in her faded bell bottom jeans, oh so perfectly frayed along the edges. Margo preferred denim overalls and red bandanas. Nancy liked tiny skirts with ballet flats. And Monica, with her long, straight hair parted in the middle, so reminiscent of Stephen Stills' erstwhile girlfriend Judy Collins—she was partial to baggy jeans and embroidered Mexican shirts.

They traveled in a pack and had this way of walking four abreast that made them seem invincible. Lethally beautiful. Like the alpha girls or mean girls of today. Were they mean? I don't have a clue. I was too afraid to approach them.

But I do know how they made me feel. Exactly like the speaker of that song: "Helplessly hoping...gasping at glimpses—wishing I could fly, only to trip at the sound of goodbye." And it wasn't just that song. It was all the songs on that album, so achingly beautiful, including his famous break-up song for Judy Collins: "Sometimes it hurts so badly I must cry out loud...I am lonely..."

At the time, it was an excruciating amount of emotion to bear. So, I did the only thing my teenage self knew how to do. I decided that I hated Monica, Margo, Nancy and Barbara—and also Crosby, Stills and Nash. And later Young. All those saccharine melodies and sentimental lyrics. Ugh! I preferred the Rolling Stones and Jimi Hendrix and the Grateful Dead.

Yet, fifty years later, I discovered that those very same songs had the power to move me. To fill me with an unsettled longing and a touch of dread and sorrow. Only this time around, it wasn't painful. It didn't bother me. I just thought they were beautiful.

And I began to wonder, what if I was wrong about everything? Wrong about Stephen Stills. Wrong about Crosby, Stills, and Nash, and later Young. Wrong about Monica, Margo, Nancy and Barbara. Maybe they weren't as invincible as I thought they were. I began to wonder what happened to them after high school. How it all worked out for them. But I resisted the temptation to go online and find out.

ART BELL

Art Bell is a graduate of Lakewood High School in Lakewood, New Jersey. After graduating from Swarthmore College, he worked as an economist in Washington DC, then decided to pursue a career in television. He has worked at CBS, HBO (where he founded Comedy Central), Comedy Central, and Court TV. Art lives in Larchmont, NY with his wife, Carrie. He is currently writing a memoir about Comedy Central.

A FEW MINOR ALTERATIONS

Art Bell

I started trumpet lessons in fifth grade; by high school, I was good enough to play in the marching band.

Our first band rehearsal was on the football field under a blazing late-August sun. There were fifty-four of us, all in sweat-soaked shorts and T-shirts, all hot and tired before we even started. I held a soggy mimeographed sheet diagramming where my "squad" of four trumpeters would march so that the band spelled out "LHS" (for Lakewood High School) in giant human letters as we played the school fight song, "On for Lakewood." By late afternoon, we were overheated and sunburned crimson. I thought we'd never get it right, but finally everything clicked into place and after the band formed those giant letters on the field, we were allowed to go home.

We got our band uniforms when school started a week later. The jacket and pants were deep blue trimmed in white—our school colors. There were white leather spats that buckled over shoes, and striped suspenders that crossed in back. And, to top it off, a foot-high furry blue hat with a chinstrap. It looked like the Bride of Frankenstein's hairdo, dyed velvety blue. I hoped the hat might make me look taller, and I needed all the help I could get since I was the shortest kid in the freshman class.

Because I was so short, I worried that the uniform might not fit. As soon as Mr. Unger, our band director, handed it to me, I fished around inside the jacket to check the size: XXS, the smallest high school band uniform made. I took the uniform, hat, spats and suspenders home, ran upstairs to the privacy of my bedroom, and put everything on. The pants were so big that I could hold the waist six inches from my body. I looked at myself in the mirror; the jacket seemed to swallow me whole, and the sleeves hung down to my knees. With the suspenders and spats, it looked like I was wearing a clown suit. The only thing missing was the big red nose.

It was a week before the first game, enough time to make alterations, but my mother didn't sew, and I was too embarrassed to ask anyone else to do it. I found a box of safety pins and began the process of pulling, folding, and pinning the uniform into a wearable size. I shortened the pants and sleeves and I pulled in the waist so that it could be belted without bagging. When I finished, I climbed into the uniform, careful to avoid all the safety pins holding the excess fabric in check, and stood at the mirror. The pants and sleeves were the right length, but the jacket drooped and draped as if it hung on a tiny clothes hanger. The pants crotch hung well below my actual crotch and the zipper fly looked about two feet long. I swallowed hard and turned away from the mirror, knowing there was nothing more I could do.

On game day, uniformed and holding my fuzzy blue hat, my father drove me in silence to the high school. "See if you can get a ride home," he said as I climbed out of the car, struggling with all that pinned excess yardage. Walking down the hall to the band room, my pants broadcast a "swish, swish" sound and I braced myself for withering looks and cruel laughter.

But when I walked into the band room, no one seemed to care that I looked like Bozo the Trumpeter. A few people said hi to me as we all got our music and instruments ready. Even though I felt like the sour note in the opening chord, I began to relax, and to think that maybe I belonged. Even though the uniform didn't fit—I fit in.'

MERCY TULLIS-BUKHARI

Mercy Tullis-Bukhari is a poet, essayist, and fiction writer who finds inspiration from being a Bronx-bred Afro-Latina, Honduran and Garifuna of Jamaican descent. She is a Callaloo Fellow, and has performed at various venues throughout New York, including the Bronx Library Center, the Bowery Poetry Club, the Nuyorican Poets Café, and the Caribbean Cultural Theatre. Her first book of poems, *Smoke*, can be found on Amazon. She is currently writing her novel through the MFA program at The College of New Rochelle.

SPANISH 1

Mercy Tullis-Bukhari

On my first day of Spanish 1 at Cardinal Spellman High School in the Northeast section of The Bronx, the teacher asked the class if anyone spoke Spanish at home. Three of us raised our hands. I am dark-skinned with kinky hair, and the other two girls had light brown complexions with loosely curled hair.

She asked the three of us to approach her desk. Without asking us any questions about our background, she immediately sent the other two girls to the foreign language department to request a transfer to an advanced Spanish class. I, however, was told to sit back down.

The term "Afro Latinidad" has recently become a common term in discussions of ethnicity. My Afro Latinidad is defined by being from Honduras, and of Garifuna and Jamaican descent. Both of my parents were born in Honduras, Central America, and they are both Black. I grew up eating tortillas with fried eggs, refried beans, and crema for breakfast. I grew up listening to salsa, hip hop, and the Honduran-Garifuna traditional music called punta. I grew up with my mother speaking only Spanish to me. I never had to think about my Latinidad and Blackness because both managed to coexist in my home without constrictions and explanations.

When the Spanish teacher told me to sit back down, I was confused. My upbringing and my Catholic schooling taught me to trust my teachers, but the Spanish teacher's immediate dismissal unsettled me in a way I could not articulate as a high school freshman. I felt embarrassed because all the students in the class saw me walk to the teacher's desk with the two light-complexioned students, then watched me sit back down by myself. What I always knew about myself—about my culture and identity—was negated by the simple act of being told to sit down.

Without a glance at my test scores or even a conversation to evaluate my proficiency, the teacher determined with a narrow white gaze that the thirteen-year-old standing before her with dark skin and kinky hair was not "Latino enough" to be transferred to an advanced Spanish class, and she told me to sit back down.

The other kids in my Spanish 1 class had absolutely no exposure to Spanish language or culture at home and the teacher's lessons consisted of how to say "Buenos Dias," "Esto es un lapiz" "Hola" "¡Adios, Hasta Pronto!" The non-Spanish speaking students responded with an American inflection.

Not me.

I never studied for a test and always scored perfectly. As you might imagine, my classmates wanted me to join in their group projects, because they knew their projects would be scored perfectly, too. It was flattering, of course, but sitting in that classroom was demeaning. I knew I was being used for my knowledge, but I was never acknowledged for it. When I spoke with the two light-complexioned girls about their advanced Spanish class, they told me how they were learning how to write research papers, and how they were speaking only Spanish in the classroom.

Not me. Not the one who lived in a conversational Spanish environment. The one whose mother only spoke Spanish to her. Who had pen pals in Honduras. Who ate tortillas and refried beans with fried eggs for breakfast. Who was obviously beyond learning how to say "¡Hola!" and "¡Hasta Pronto!" And although that Spanish teacher saw the effortless grades I produced, she never considered moving me forward.

Ultimately, I spent my four years at Cardinal Spellman High School not identifying myself in any way. I had no language. I had no culture. I had no hip hop or tortillas, no punta or crema. Me sentia como un barco sin pasajeros, navegando en el gran océano—I felt like a boat, aimlessly floating on water, without passengers—floating through my Spanish class and around my high school building without anyone knowing who I am.

SUSIE ORMAN SCHNALL

Susie Orman Schnall is the author of three novels: Her thought-provoking debut, On Grace, is about turning forty. *The Balance Project* is about work-life balance and was inspired by The Balance Project interview series she started in 2014. And *The Subway Girls* is historical fiction about the fascinating Miss Subways advertising program. Susie's writing has appeared in numerous publications including the *New York Times, HuffPost, POPSUGAR, Writer's Digest, Harper's Bazaar,* and *Glamour*. She is also a frequent speaker at women's groups, corporations, and book clubs about her novels and work-life balance. Susie grew up in Los Angeles, graduated from the University of Pennsylvania, and now lives in Purchase, New York, with her husband, Rick, and their three teenage sons.

MISS LANDAU

Susie Orman Schnall

I was running for student body vice president at Birmingham High School, a large public school in Los Angeles' San Fernando Valley. We had 562 kids in our class. Many were bused in from South Central. I drove in from Encino, a couple of miles away.

For the elections, I shared a ticket with Walter Martin, known as Ricky. He was a popular football player who wanted to be student body president. We called ourselves the Dream Team.

It was 1987 so naturally, I wrote my campaign speech as a rap. I performed it backed up by dancers in oversized sweatshirts and a classmate scratching records on a turntable. I still know every word. It began:

My name is Susie Orman and I'm nice and naughty
I'm running for vice president of the student body
and ended:
So if you vote for me you'll have my gratitude
And if you don't then there's a problem with your attitude

It was a moment. And we won. I would become student body vice president of Birmingham my senior year.

One of the many roles of the student body vice president was to present the "Welcome to Birmingham" speech at the fall orientation for incoming students. I looked forward to this responsibility and took it seriously. But, Miss Landau.

Oh, Miss Landau.

Miss Landau, a guidance counselor, was in charge of the incoming students' orientation. She called me into her office one day and told me she thought my voice was too high. That when I got excited, my voice got screechy and was difficult to understand. She didn't think it would depict our school in its best light. She would be asking the student body secretary to give the speech instead.

I was speechless.

The student body secretary was Jenny Donaldson, whose talents, besides being able to take comprehensive notes in legible handwriting, included, apparently, a lovely speaking voice.

I'm not sure if Miss Landau knew it at the time, but I lost my voice that day. It would take years after that disheartening meeting before I would no longer be embarrassed to introduce myself. Years before, I felt comfortable speaking in front of crowds. Years before, I didn't think that the first thing that came to someone's mind upon hearing my voice was how ridiculous it must sound. Since then, I've been told on way too many occasions that I sound just like Bart Simpson. That is so not confidence-building.

I don't remember the day of that orientation. I don't remember if I even heard how Jenny Donaldson did. If her voice was up to snuff. If Birmingham was depicted in its best light. If the parents and students in that auditorium were grateful that Jenny's voice didn't screech, that it had a pleasing tone.

I should have gotten over it by now, but there are days I'm still convinced that when I open my mouth, people snicker at what comes out. I still don't believe when friends tell me my voice is normal. I still cringe when I hear others with high-pitched or unusual voices, because I wonder if my reaction to them is the same as other people's reaction to me.

Sometimes I deepen my voice purposefully. Like I'm doing right now.

Do I sound bitter? I'm not bitter.

But thirty years after Miss Landau silenced my speech, I know now what I should have done at that orientation.

If I had the confidence back then that I do now, I would have marched into that auditorium, asked the dulcet Jenny Donaldson to please take her seat, cleared my squeaky throat and [clear throat] began:

> *My voice may be squeaky, may sound like noise*
> *But listen up you girls and boys*
> *Miss Landau came at me, filled with hate*
> *But dear Miss Landau, just you wait*
> *I earned this speech, I campaigned and fought*
> *And I'm not throwing away my shot.*

LAURENCE S. WILLIAMS

Laurence Williams writes, plays bass guitar in a classic rock band, and worked in the Bronx Supreme Court for over thirty-five years. His work has been published in *The First Line* Literary Journal and *The Middle Church Literary Magazine,* and he's a proud member of the Under the Bridge Writing Group in Tarrytown. Born and raised in the Bronx, he now resides with his wife—they're two happy empty nesters—in New City.

THE LONGEST DAY

Laurence S. Williams

The night before my first day of high school, my brother sits me down and tells me to pay attention. As the middle child of seven, I've learned to fend for myself, but he is a senior, and the third Williams to attend Cardinal Spellman High School. He never gives advice. This must be important. First, don't buy the pool pass, he says. Why? He gives me that look, the one that says you're an idiot. There is no pool. Never show your money. Not like I have a lot, but okay. Never go into the bathroom by yourself. That fills me with trepidation. Here's the biggie, he says. Something bigger than the bathroom? After gym class, walk to the showers and back with your towel slung over your shoulder. The expression on my face screams for pity. The guys that cover up are still searching for their clothes. How come I never heard this? What kind of place is this? The nuns were bad enough, but this. And, he says. You mean there's something else? If you see the dean, head the other way. Him, I've heard about.

So, I'm sitting in this giant auditorium waiting for orientation and feeling confident with my insider information, until someone grabs me by my hair and yanks my head back. The pain is excruciating but I won't give in. I'm staring into his eyes, this Beowulf, who from this angle looks seven feet tall. He growls. "What's your name?" "Laurence Williams." "Another Williams. I've got my eye on you." My bravado slides into my testicles, and I hate my brothers for pissing him off. Telling my parents is not even an option because they'll think I did something to provoke it. He lets go and strolls to the stage amidst five hundred teenagers and I can smell the fear across the room. At lunch, I locate my brother in the cafeteria and tell him what happened. The table erupts in laughter. Good, now he'll leave me alone, my brother says.

The rest of the day I'm looking over my shoulder, my stomach doing somersaults. I can't enjoy the sight of two freshmen handing over five dollars for a piece of paper proclaiming Pool Pass in block letters. After gym class, I remember my brother's warning and slink towards the showers exposed in my nakedness. I see Vinny, a friend from the neighborhood, and he's got his towel wrapped around him. I try to warn him, but it's too late. Two boys rip the towel off, stripping him of his innocence, of all our innocence. His clothes? Nobody knows what happened to them. The bathroom? I won't even tell you what goes on there. But I avoid the dean, my main objective.

It is 1972, and the world is changing at a dizzying pace. In my universe, nobody tells me what's good or bad, happy or sad, right or wrong. It is just the way things are. I have to figure it out for myself.

That day isn't all bad. I'm fourteen and it's the first time I'm around so many sixteen and seventeen-year old girls. In between periods, students hold the door open for each other like it's Mission Impossible, while they go outside and smoke. I think I even hear the theme song playing. I'm pressed into service by some juniors as they puff away, laughing and kissing, and I'm about to have an accident right there in the stairwell. I grow up that day and make my first rebellious decision that will affect the rest of my life. I will not spend four years in this place.

Finally, it's 3:00 p.m. and the most amazing thing happens. Once I turn the corner, the school doesn't care anymore. Kids are smoking dope, selling drugs, mooning people from the bus, getting into fights. But I'm off school grounds. I am society's problem now.

JESSICA RAO

Jessica Rao has done just about every kind of writing there is. She has been an award-winning business contributor at CNBC.com and a lifestyle writer for Gannett. She has written magazine articles, blog posts and three schoolbooks published by McGraw Hill. She's has even taught writing to high school students and has run her own PR firm. These days, as a mom of two, Jessica needs a few more hours on any given day, and she blogs about it at TimeInsensitive.com. Jessica is also a student at The Writing Institute of Sarah Lawrence College, where she is workshopping a novel about a nineteen-year-old Brooklyn girl who drops out of school to become a waitress.

BALL GIRL

Jessica Rao

Growing up, you might have called me a ball girl. Not the kind that retrieves discarded baseball bats, but the kind of girl who loved to play ball. The summer before my freshman year in high school, I attended sleepaway camp. Every night after dinner, I played basketball with the boys. I learned to fake left and drive right and sink baseline jump shots. Along with my many thirteen year old crushes, I fell in love with the sound of the ball dropping through the net.

That fall, I tried out for my high school basketball team. The Monday after tryouts, I ran to check the junior varsity list. My name wasn't there. I scanned the varsity roster, and at the bottom, found my name. I had made the team ahead of sophomores and juniors. I was never so excited about anything in my life, probably because I hadn't kissed a boy yet.

During the first days of practice, no one knew my name. I watched the older girls. Heard the nicknames they used. Sat among them on the team van. I was far more interested in what our coach was writing on his clipboard than what any of my teachers were writing on the blackboard. And being on varsity became part of my identity. In my yearbook that spring, the team captain wrote, "Yo All-Star! Glad you were on the team!"

In my sophomore year, the varsity coach moved away. The junior varsity coach took over. At tryouts, there were new drills and new faces. This year, I thought, I'm going to get *really* good.

After tryouts, I went to the varsity list to see who my teammates would be. I didn't see my name. I looked again. It wasn't there. I looked down the junior varsity roster and there, under "R," was Jessica Rao. Things went gray. I ran to the pay phone to call my parents. *How dare that ogre-coach pick those other girls over me? Wasn't she watching?*

I didn't want to go to school but the next day my father, who had never gone to talk to a teacher before, called the coach and asked for an appointment. On a cold day, the two of us walked from the academic building to the gym. We found the coaches laughing in the office. My dad went inside, but when he came out, he looked upset. "She won't change your spot."

I wanted to quit, but I still wanted to play. "You *should* still play," my Dad said. "It doesn't matter what team you are on. Just do the best you can." That season, I was the junior varsity captain and the leading scorer. Whenever Coach C was around, I looked the other way.

I no longer play basketball. I'm lucky if I make it to the gym. And I had all but forgotten my sophomore year disappointment until a Facebook message from Coach C landed in my inbox.

Jessica,

I want to apologize for the big mistake I made cutting you from varsity when you were at school. In retrospect, you would have risen to the occasion without a hitch. You were so gung-ho about basketball. I still remember.

I've lived with this for a long time and am pleased to finally get the chance to say how sorry I am to have burst your bubble. I did the wrong thing all those years ago.

As I read her words, tears rolled down my face. I cried for the fourteen-year-old I'd been, for how she'd changed from a ball girl to a grownup. I cried for Coach C who carried this with her all these years. And as I blotted those tears, I felt grateful that the same excited freshman girl still shows up every now and then—when my fingers are tapping the keyboard, when I'm with my family, and yes, when I'm cheering my own kids on the basketball court.

LYNN EDELSON

Lynn Edelson is a special educator and family trainer in the New York State Early Intervention Program. She is the mother of two grown sons, a writer and a musician, and is fairly certain neither one will ever buy her a beach house. For the past five years, she has studied memoir at The Writing Institute at Sarah Lawrence College. Though she has often been accused of writing poetry, she is currently at work on a collection of short stories. In May 2016, her essay, *Heart Monitor*, was selected to be part of the NYC *Listen To Your Mother* show. Lynn lives in the Hudson Valley with her husband, Michael Principe, and Sadie (aka The Bad Dog of Brewster).

THE MAILBOX

Lynn Edelson

She moved our seats after the first few weeks of school.

I had been happy sitting near the girls I knew and passing notes during tenth grade world history. Mrs. Gallagher never said a word about it, but on that Monday, she announced there would be some changes.

Assigned seats, kiddos.

She pointed me towards a desk in the front row, next to a boy dressed in black. His long legs sprawled near the chair that was to be mine.

John, she said. *Move over.*

Yeah, he said as he pulled in his leg.

I stood as far away from him as our touching desks would allow and nodded hello.

Hey, he said.

He was one of the guys who smoked Marlboros near the blue mailbox across the street from the school and catcalled the girls who walked by.

Nice, baby, they cooed.

We all wore skirts back then, with tights or knee socks and penny loafers. The girls with teased hair wore stockings with their white sneakers, and they were as tough as the boys.

Fuck you, they'd say to the guys as they walked by.

I said nothing and tried to avoid the mailbox.

I sat down at the desk, turned my body away from his, and accidentally grazed his leg. I flinched and quickly pulled away.

Relax honey, he said under his breath.

In time I did relax, and in time I did what I do.

Nice sweater, I said as I glanced at the black cardigan covering his tailored white shirt.

You like it?

Great color, I said. *Matches your pants.*

He closed his eyes halfway and smiled.

Just for you, baby.

His long black hair was slicked back and reached past his collar.

He began to tease me back.

How are all your girlfriends? he said in that low voice.

Way too smart for you, I answered.

I was college track. He was one of the Greasers, the ones going nowhere. They were the kids who drank and used drugs, and wore black leather jackets and pointy black boots, and something about those bad boys caught my eye. Not the stupid ones, but the ones like him who were smoldering with something else.

John, Mrs. Gallagher would say. *What's the answer?*

And he'd talk in that low quiet voice that made her smile.

She knew what we did not.

That he was as smart as any kid taking the regents exams.

He would become an attorney.

At the twenty-year reunion, the girls who had never looked at him couldn't keep their eyes off of him. He was tall, slender, funny and gorgeous.

You look like shit, I told him.

I just got out of the hospital, he said. Kidney stone.

I pulled out a chair and pointed to it. Sit down, you idiot.

He smiled that smile with his eyes half closed.

At the 40-year reunion, I almost didn't recognize him. He was heavier and grayer and now a popular legislator. He was the local celebrity, and everyone wanted his attention.

I didn't think he remembered me, and I couldn't bear having to remind him of how we had sat close enough to touch.

When it was time to take the group picture on the dance floor at the end of the night, I felt a hand on my shoulder. Over here, he said, guiding me towards the edge of the crowd.

I stood next to him, and as I smiled that awful smile of reunion photos, I muttered through my teeth, *I cannot believe you're a Republican.*

Oh, you must be a Democrat, he said. He smiled broadly, nodding at those who waved to him across the room.

You are such a politician, I said. *And I would always vote for the other guy.*

Oh, you'd vote for me honey, he said softly as he leaned down to kiss me goodbye.

EDWARD McCANN

Edward McCann is an award winning writer/producer and the founder and editor of **650**, a literary forum that celebrates the spoken word with live events in New York City and elsewhere. A longtime contributing editor to *Country Living*, his features and essays have been published in many literary journals, anthologies, and national magazines, including *Milieu, Better Homes & Gardens, Good Housekeeping, The Irish Echo, The Sun, and others*. His essay, "Pregnant Again," was selected for the anthology, *Listen To Your Mother*, published by Penguin, and he's recently completed a memoir about the search for his missing nephew. A member of New York City-based Artists Without Walls, he lives and writes in New York's Hudson River Valley.

ACKNOWLEDGMENTS

In addition to the contributors to this volume, we thank the **New Rochelle Council on the Arts** for its generous support of 650, and for stimulating and encouraging the study and presentation of the performing and fine arts. Throughout the year, NRCA sponsors many exhibitions, theatrical productions, dance recitals, film screenings, lectures, and concert series. **NewRochelleArts.org**

We thank **The New Rochelle Public Library** for its generous support of 650, and for stimulating and encouraging the study and presentation of the performing and fine arts. Throughout the year, NRCA sponsors many exhibitions, theatrical productions, dance recitals, film screenings, lectures, and concert series. **NRPL.org**

In addition to the contributors to this volume, we thank **Nancy Manocherian's** *the cell,* which supported 650 at its inception. A twenty-first century salon in the heart of New York City, their mission is to support the arts and to incubate new works, and the cell made its beautiful performance space available to 650 as we were finding our way. The cell: To mine the mind, pierce the heart, and awaken the soul. **TheCellTheatre.org**

Artists Without Walls was created to inspire, uplift and unite people and communities of diverse cultures through the pursuit of artistic achievement, and has supported and encouraged 650 from its beginnings. Artists Without Walls: No Limits. No Walls. No Boundaries. **ArtistsWithoutWalls.com**

READ650.COM

INFO @READ650.COM
FACEBOOK.COM/READ650

www.ingramcontent.com/pod-product-compliance
Lightning Source LLC
Chambersburg PA
CBHW072042170626
46811CB00008B/3127